TEENAGE MUTANT NINJA TURTLES
ABC's
for a Better Planet

By J. K. Rosser
Illustrated by The GEE Studio

Based on the Teenage Mutant Ninja Turtles characters and
comic books created by Kevin Eastman and Peter Laird

A Random House PICTUREBACK®

Random House 🏠 New York

Library of Congress Cataloging-in-Publication Data
Rosser, J. K. Teenage mutant ninja turtles ABC's for a better planet / by J. K. Rosser ; illustrated by the GEE Studio. p.   cm.–(A Random House pictureback) "Based on the teenage mutant ninja turtles characters and comic books created by Kevin Eastman and Peter Laird." SUMMARY: The renowned warrior turtles use the alphabet to inform readers of the problems of pollution and environmental degradation, and what children can do to help protect the environment and the Earth's resources. ISBN 0-679-81383-7 (pbk.)–ISBN 0-679-91383-1 (lib. bdg.) 1. Environmental protection–Citizen participation–Juvenile literature. [1. Environmental protection. 2. Alphabet.] I. Eastman, Kevin B., ill. II. GEE Studio. III. Title. TD171.7.R67   1991   363.7–dc20   [E] 90-53247 CIP AC

Manufactured in the United States of America   10 9 8 7 6 5 4 3 2 1

Introduction

Hey, dudes! Ever stop and look around at this earth? On a totally awesome day, the sky is blue...and flowers are blooming...and the air smells great. But what's *really* happening to the planet?

Have you heard people talking about acid rain? The greenhouse effect? The ozone layer? Do you know what the words mean? We're here to tell you—and to show how you can pitch in to help save our planet from some of the bad things that are happening to it.

A is for Acid rain

Smoke and car-exhaust fumes give off certain gases. The gases rise into the air and mix with water. That makes dilute acid, which sometimes falls back to earth as rain or snow. This "acid rain" pollutes rivers and kills fish and trees. It's even eating away buildings and some monuments and ancient statues.

What can you do? Save energy—use less electricity. When you use less electricity, less coal is burned to make power plants run. Use the car less. Ride a bike whenever you can instead of driving in a car.

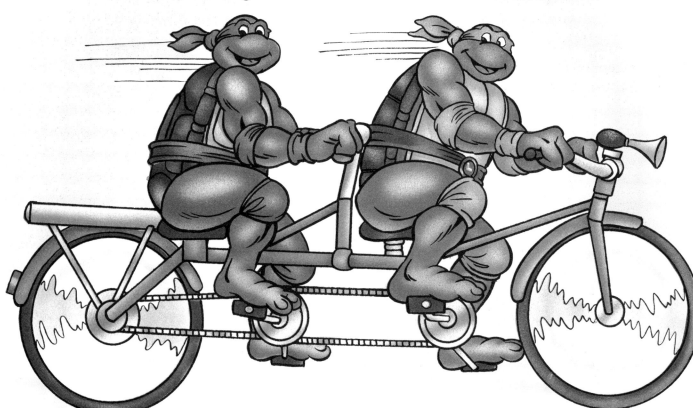

B is for Batteries

Batteries are cheap and easy to use—especially if you like music wherever you go! But when it comes time to throw them out, watch out! Many batteries have mercury in them, which is poisonous. Batteries are dangerous if they leak. And it takes a lot of energy to manufacture a battery—up to 50 times more energy than it takes to power your portable radio.

What can you do? Buy mercury-free batteries and ask your friends to do the same. Use rechargeable batteries whenever you can, so each one lasts longer. And better still—don't use too many batteries in the first place.

C is for Cruelty-free products

Lots of products have to be tested by scientists before people can use them. Sometimes the products—like shampoo or make-up—are tested on animals in laboratories. The tests are cruel to the lab animals, and the animals can't fight back. Besides, testing on animals sometimes doesn't prove anything. What works one way on animals may not work the same way on humans.

What can you do? Buy products that are labeled "cruelty-free."

D is for Dolphins

Dolphins are one of the smartest species on the planet. They're friendly, too. But did you know that thousands of them die each year when they get trapped in tuna fishermen's nets? This happens mostly in the eastern Pacific Ocean.

What can you do? Buy tuna that says "Dolphin-free" on the label. Or write to the canned tuna-fish manufacturers and find out where and how they catch their tuna. Don't buy tuna if dolphins had to die too!

E is for Extinction and Endangered species

When all the animals or plants in a species are no longer alive, that species has become *extinct*. If the animals or plants are dying off, the species is *endangered*. Dodo birds and dinosaurs, for example, are now extinct. Other animals, like elephants and rhinos, are now endangered. They're dying off because humans kill them or harm their environments.

What can you do? Don't give or accept souvenirs made from plants or animals that are endangered— such as souvenirs made from ivory, coral, reptile skins, and of course, turtle shells!

F is for Fast Food

Fast food tastes pretty good, but it's not very good for you. Most of it is fried, and seasoned with too much salt or sweetened with sugar. Some of it even contains chemical additives. And the Styrofoam dishes contain chlorofluorocarbons (we call 'em CFCs for short), which pollute the atmosphere.

What can you do? We're not asking you to stop eating fast food. But don't eat too much of it too often. And don't give your business to fast-food places that serve their stuff in Styrofoam.

G is for Greenhouse effect

Our planet is heating up too fast—and *that's* not cool! The sun warms the land and water, and energy is reflected to the layers of gases above the earth. The gases—like carbon dioxide—absorb the energy and trap heat. That's important, because we need heat to live.

But power plants, cars, and factories give off new gases every day. These gases trap even more heat. They create a sort of giant greenhouse over the earth. This greenhouse effect produces floods (from melting polar icecaps), droughts (which hurt crops), and storms. And the more gases we release into the air, the worse the greenhouse effect becomes.

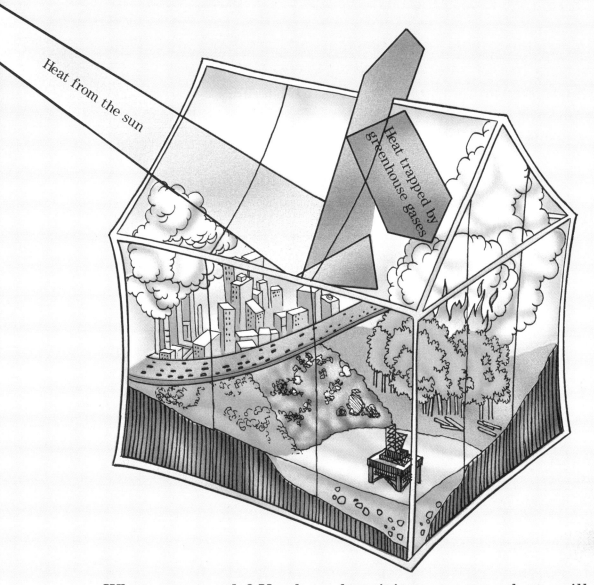

What can you do? Use less electricity, so power plants will burn less fuel. Take fewer car trips. Car-exhaust fumes contain carbon dioxide. And—most important—don't use Styrofoam or aerosol spray cans. They both contain CFCs.

H is for Hazardous waste in your Home

Remember that toxic mutagen slime that changed us into mutant turtles? Well, hazardous waste is awful and dangerous. In fact, we four guys are the only good things that ever came out of it! Spilled paint, motor oil, or gasoline can pollute thousands of gallons of water if it seeps into the ground.

What can you do? Try not to create so much garbage, first of all. Don't buy things like pens and cameras and flashlights that are advertised as "disposable." And don't let your folks throw cans of oil, paint, and gasoline in the trash. Keep those materials separate, to be picked up specially for a toxic-waste collection site.

I is for Ivory

Ivory is beautiful. But it comes from elephant tusks, which means that elephants are killed for the ivory.

What can you do? Don't give or accept things made of ivory. If no one wants the ivory, elephants won't be killed so often.

The more the merrier, dudes! Join a group to fight for our planet. Start a recycling collection, write to your city's mayor, go to an Earth Day rally.

Keep informed about what's good for you and your planet and what's not. Read articles and books about the environment. Keep alert. Read labels to see what ingredients are in your food. Get together with your family and friends to talk about ways to help the planet. Right now, it's the only one we've got. Let's keep it looking radical!

L is for Litter

Litter is a drag to look at and a pain to clean up.

What can you do? First of all—don't litter! Put your trash in wastebaskets (even little bits like gum wrappers). Take stuff that can be recycled, like soda cans, to a recycling center or back to the store. It's up to everyone to pitch in— so pitch your litter into the trash can, not onto the ground! And you know those plastic rings that hold soda six-packs together? If they get washed out to sea, birds and sea creatures can strangle in them. So cut through the rings before you throw them away in the trash.

M is for Meat

Some animals are injected with artificial hormones to make them grow faster. But some of these hormones cause cancer. A lot of the world's cereal crop is fed to cattle, when it could be used to feed starving people instead. And cattle expel methane, a gas that makes the greenhouse effect worse.

What can you do? How about not eating so much meat in the first place? And ask your folks to buy meat from organically raised beef cattle.

N is for Newspapers

Newspaper is made from trees. (That includes the comics, too!) When trees are cut down, there are fewer around to absorb carbon dioxide, another gas that makes the greenhouse effect worse.

What can you do? Save trees. Old newspapers can be used to make new newspapers. So recycle them! Stack them in bundles tied with twine. Maybe your neighborhood has a weekly pickup of newspapers right at the street curb. If not, find out where the nearest recycling center or collection point is—and get your bundles over there!

O is for Ozone layer

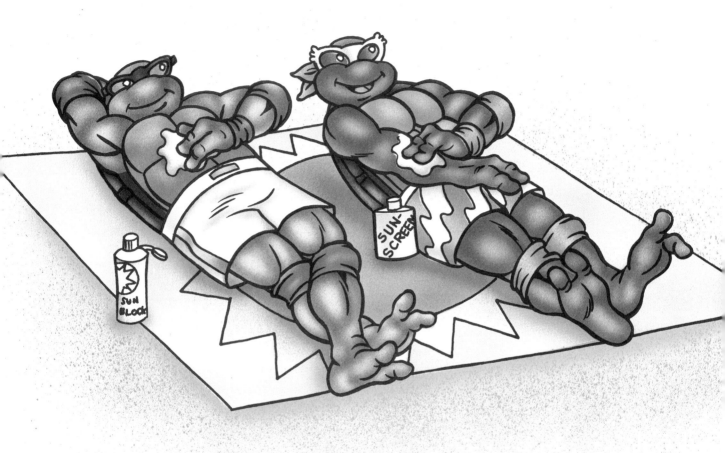

The sun is good. But the sun's ultraviolet rays can cause eye diseases and skin cancer in people. They can also harm crops and kill ocean plankton. The ozone layer protects us from the sun's deadly radiation. This layer is made up of gases miles above the earth. But the ozone layer is getting thinner each year.

What can you do? Protect yourself. Wear sunglasses and sunscreen. Protect the ozone, too. Don't use aerosol spray cans. CFCs are the gases used to push stuff out of aerosol spray cans. Reduce your use of home and car air conditioners, which also use CFCs. And CFCs destroy the ozone layer in a *big* way. Even if everyone stopped using CFCs today, those already in the atmosphere would still be around for another *hundred* years! So the sooner we stop using CFCs, the better.

P is for Pesticides

Pesticides are chemical poisons used by farmers to kill weeds and insect pests. But some pesticides are still in the food when it gets to the supermarket. And pesticides also poison animals that *aren't* pests.

What can you do? Get your folks to buy fruits and vegetables that are grown organically—that is, without chemical pesticides. Organically grown stuff may not look as perfect, but it tastes great—and it's good for you.

Q is for Questions

Always ask questions! How was this product made? Do I really need it? Was it tested on animals? When I'm done with it, how do I get rid of it without hurting the earth? Can it be recycled or used again?

R is for Remember to Recycle Rubbish

Remember, the planet is not a giant garbage can. If we don't start recycling, we'll soon run out of room for storing our garbage. And methane, a greenhouse-effect gas, is released into the air as garbage rots.

What can you do? Do your folks have a garden? Start a compost heap for food scraps. Return soda cans and bottles to the store for a refund on your deposit. Reuse paper whenever you can (the backs of envelopes or the clean backs of notebook sheets are great for scrap paper). Reuse plastic containers. Bring newspapers, glass jars, and aluminum cans to your neighborhood recycling center.

S is for Seals

Seals are in danger, just like dolphins. When certain chemicals, such as polychlorinated biphenyls (we call 'em PCBs for short), get into the seas, they pollute fish. When seals eat the polluted fish, they get sick and die. If something isn't done soon about PCBs in the oceans, many wild sea mammals, including seals, will become extinct.

What can you do? Support or join groups that are fighting for cleaner seas. Clean up litter that you find at the beach so it doesn't go out with the tide.

T is for Tropical rain forests

The tropical rain forests are a green belt running across the equator. Up to half of *all* living things live in the rain forests, including plants used to make medicines. But the forests are being destroyed—about 90 *million* acres every year! Trees are cut down for timber, or burned to clear land for raising cattle or crops, even though the soil isn't very good for farming.

What can you do? Learn more about the rain forests and the people, plants, and animals in them. Don't buy anything made of tropical woods, like teak or mahogany or rosewood.

U is for Unleaded gas

When your folks "fill 'er up" at the gas station, they probably buy unleaded gas. The lead that used to be in gasoline produced dioxins. Dioxins are dangerous chemicals that cause cancer and birth defects in animals.

V is for Volunteer to clean up

It's easy to *say* "Let's save the tropical rain forests," or
"Let's clean up the oceans," but it's hard for a kid to *do*.
So, what about making your own neighborhood a better
place to live? Start close to home: Volunteer to clean up
your local park or beach. Pick up litter, or help with some
gardening (like weeding and pruning). Get a group of kids
together, to make it even more fun!

W is for Whales

Save them! Some species of whale, like the giant blue whale, are now endangered. Whales have been hunted for so many years that hunting them is no longer allowed– except in Norway and Japan, where whales are hunted for what the hunters call "scientific" reasons.

What can you do? Join a group. Learn all you can about whales and how to help save them.

X is for X-rays

X-rays are good to have when you need them—like if your doctor thinks your arm may be broken, or if the dentist wants to check for hidden cavities. But the radiation in x-rays may be harmful, especially if you have many of them over a period of time.

What can you do? Avoid x-rays unless they're really necessary. And always ask for a lead shield if the doctor or dentist doesn't put one on you before taking the x-ray.

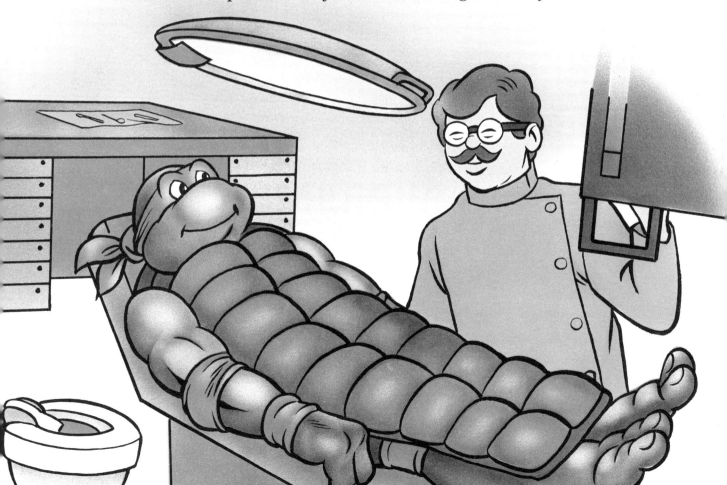

Y is for You

You can make a difference!
Write to your government
leaders at every level—city,
county, state, and federal.

Don't buy or use products that hurt
the environment. Get your folks
and friends to do the same.

Look back through this book to see other things you can do to be our favorite color–*green.*

Being green means being more in tune with the earth!

Z is for Zoos

Zoos are fun to visit. Did you know they're important, too? Zoos can help save endangered species. So support your local zoo (and remember to always obey the signs!).